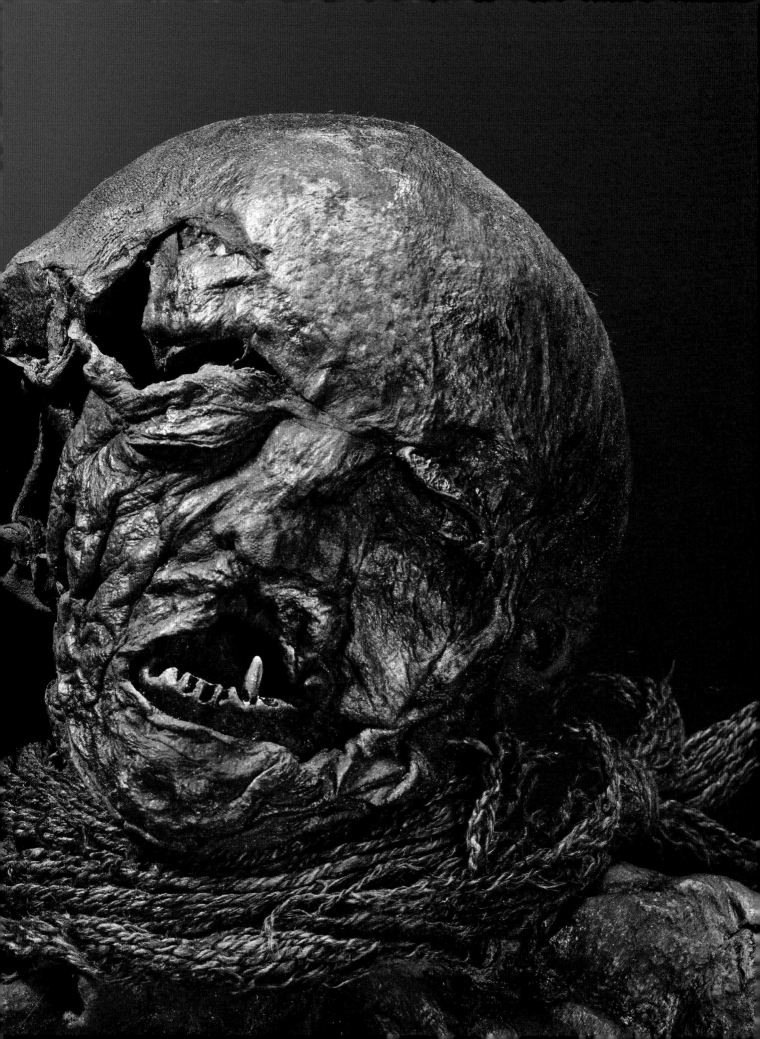

MUMMIES

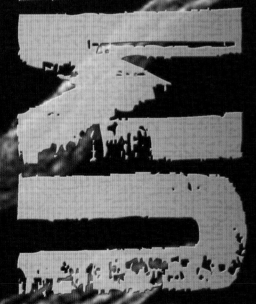

DRIED, TANNED
SEALED,
DRAINED, FROZEN,
EMBALMED,
STUFFED, WRAPPED,
AND SMOKED...

AND
WE'RE
DEAD
SERIOUS

BY CHRISTOPHER SLOAN

NATIONAL
GEOGRAPHIC
Washington, D.C.

Published by the National Geographic Society

John M. Fahey, Jr.,
President and Chief Executive Officer

Gilbert M. Grosvenor,
Chairman of the Board

Tim T. Kelly,
President, Global Media Group

John Q. Griffin,
*Executive Vice President;
President, Publishing*

Nina D. Hoffman,
*Executive Vice President,
President of Book Publishing Group*

Melina Gerosa Bellows,
*Executive Vice President of
Children's Publishing*

Staff for This Book

Robin Terry,
Project Editor

David M. Seager,
Art Director

Lori Epstein,
Illustrations Editor

Kate Olesin,
Editorial Assistant

The M Factory,
Map Research & Production

Grace Hill,
Associate Managing Editor

Lewis R. Bassford,
Production Manager

Susan Borke,
Legal and Business Affairs

Prepared by the Book Division

Nancy Laties Feresten,
*Vice President, Editor in Chief,
Children's Books*

Jonathan Halling,
*Design Director,
Children's Publishing*

Jennifer Emmett,
*Executive Editor,
Reference and Solo, Children's Books*

Carl Mehler,
Director of Maps

R. Gary Colbert,
Production Director

Jennifer A. Thornton,
Managing Editor

Manufacturing and Quality Management

Christopher A. Liedel,
Chief Financial Officer

Phillip L. Schlosser,
Vice President

Chris Brown,
Technical Director

Nicole Elliott,
Manufacturing Manager

Rachel Faulise,
Manufacturing Manager

Founded in 1888, the National Geographic Society is one of the largest nonprofit scientific and educational organizations in the world. It reaches more than 285 million people worldwide each month through its official journal, National Geographic, and its four other magazines; the National Geographic Channel; television documentaries; radio programs; films; books; videos and DVDs; maps; and interactive media. National Geographic has funded more than 8,000 scientific research projects and supports an education program combating geographic illiteracy.

For more information, please call 1-800-NGS LINE (647-5463) or write to the following address:
National Geographic Society
1145 17th Street N.W.
Washington, D.C. 20036-4688
U.S.A.

Visit the Society's Web site:
nationalgeographic.com
Visit us online:
nationalgeographic.com/books.

For librarians and teachers:
ngchildrensbooks.org

More for kids from National Geographic:
kids.nationalgeographic.com

For information about special discounts for bulk purchases, please contact National Geographic Books Special Sales: ngspecsales@ngs.org

For rights or permissions inquiries, please contact National Geographic Books Subsidiary Rights:
ngbookrights@ngs.org

Library of Congress Cataloging-in-Publication Data

Sloan, Christopher.
Mummies / By Chris Sloan.
    p. cm.
Includes bibliographical references and index.
ISBN 978-1-4263-0695-2 (hardcover : alk. paper) -- ISBN 978-1-4263-0696-9 (library binding : alk. paper)
 1. Mummies--Juvenile literature. I. Title.
GN293.S56 2010
393'.3--dc22

2010008498

Printed in China

10/RRDS/1

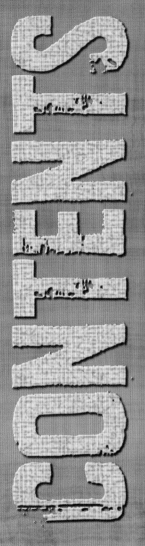

CONTENTS

ANCIENT TREASURES

If you were a powerful person who lived in the grasslands of Russia about 2,500 years ago, it is very likely that after you died, your guts would be removed from your body, your eyes would be plucked from their sockets, and your brains would be scooped out. Then you would be stuffed. This special treatment may sound like a form of punishment, but it was actually a sign of love and respect. Your body probably would be put on public display before being buried in an elaborate tomb along with your favorite possessions.

If you were a criminal or a victim of human sacrifice in Ireland at about the same time, you might have met a very different death. You might have been slashed with a sword or knife, had your head chopped off and your body cut in half, and been tossed into a marshy bog.

We know about these ancient deaths by studying two mummies, nicknamed the "Siberian Ice Maiden" and the "Oldcroghan Man." These are only two of thousands of mummies being studied in museums and science laboratories. Thousands more lie undisturbed in tombs, crypts, and graves all over the world.

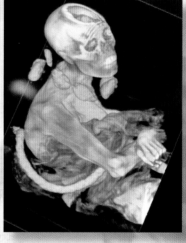

MUMMY SCIENCE
Researchers investigate the 530-year-old frozen mummy of an Inca girl (right), discovered in the Andes Mountains of Peru in 1995. A high-tech x-ray called a CT scan (inset) provides a 3-D look inside the mummy.

That may sound like a lot of mummies, but compared to the billions of people who have lived and died on Earth, mummies are actually quite rare.

Why do mummies matter? Because they still have skin, flesh, internal organs, fingernails, or hair. From these tissues we ▶

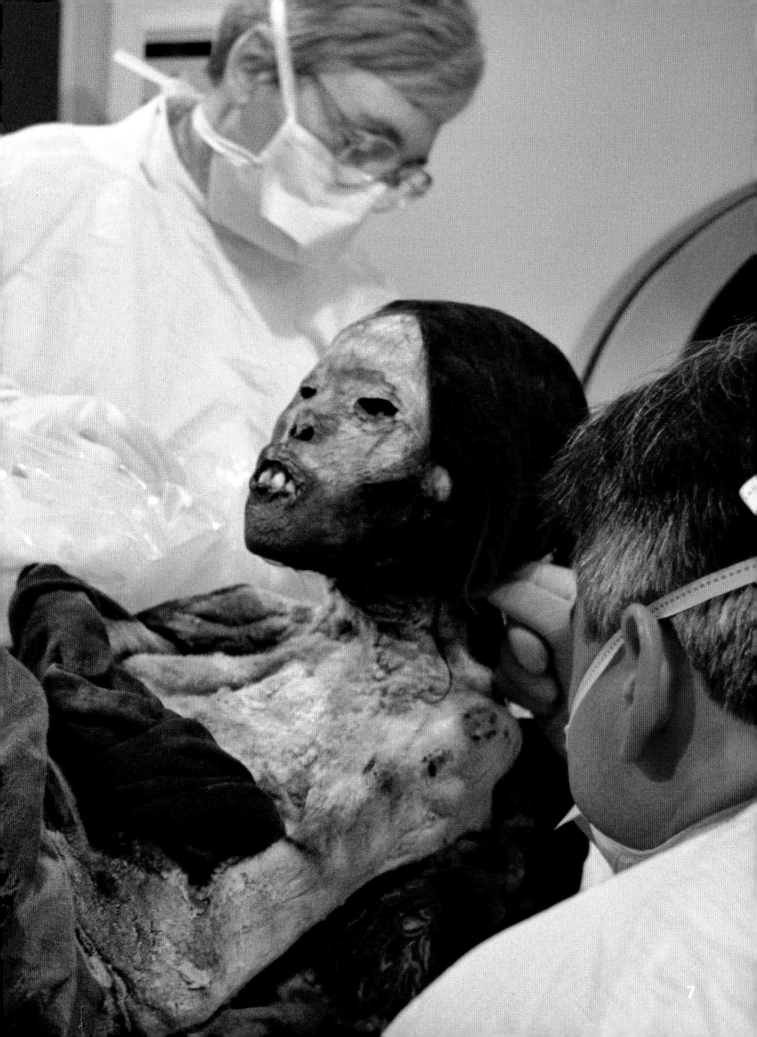

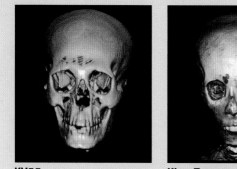

KV55   King Tut

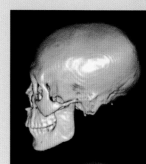

KV55   King Tut

TUT'S FAMILY PHOTOS
Researchers have long suspected that the royal mummy known as KV55, shown in a CT scanning machine (above), is King Tut's father. CT scans (left) showed that the two men had similar, unusually shaped heads. KV55 was found in the early 1900s. About a hundred years later, DNA tests finally provided scientific evidence that they are likely father and son.

can learn about the age, health, and diet of people who lived in the past. And often objects placed nearby—such as clothing, plant material, and food—are preserved as well, providing even more clues to life in ancient times. Unfortunately, once they are dug up, the delicate tissues of mummies crumble. Unless the bodies receive special care, valuable information about our past can be lost forever.

A body starts to decay a few days after death. Skin starts to turn green and the corpse begins to bloat and smell. These are signs that bacteria have moved in and begun their job of decomposing the body, taking it apart and returning its nutrients to the environment, where other living things can use it.

Mummies are different. In these bodies, the natural process of decay has been halted. Some corpses are preserved by people, usually as part of a cultural ritual. Others are preserved naturally in places where bacteria that assist decay can't live—including extremely dry climates such as deserts, cold environments such as snowy mountaintops, or in wet places with little oxygen, such as bogs.

Mummification is different from a form of temporary preservation called embalming, which slows decay for a while until a burial can be arranged. Most embalmed bodies eventually decompose, unless their embalming is repeatedly refreshed or the body is naturally preserved by the environment in which it was buried.

Whether mummies were kings and queens entombed with exotic riches, or just regular people, each body has a story to tell. By listening to these stories, told through the work of scientists, we can get close to people who lived before us. This is why mummies may be the world's most valuable ancient treasures.

STUFFED

THE MUMMY COAST

The Chinchorro people lived in the desert along the coast of northern Chile (right), where the area's few rivers meet the sea. Little did the Chinchorro know that the rivers' precious freshwater could be deadly. They mummified its child victims, like this one (above).

THE WORLD'S FIRST MUMMIES

Seven thousand years ago in the Atacama Desert of northern Chile, one of the driest places on Earth, something was killing the children of the Chinchorro people. The discovery of more than a hundred child mummies tipped off researchers that this ancient community may have suffered a terrible tragedy. When the investigators heard that the drinking water in a nearby modern town was contaminated with a deadly poison called arsenic, they had a clue to what killed those children long ago.

Researchers checked samples of the Chinchorro mummies' hair—which they knew would contain traces of the chemicals the children ate or drank—and found extremely high arsenic levels.

The mystery was solved. Arsenic occurs naturally in the soil where the Chinchorro people lived. At that time, no one knew that the odorless poison was being washed into the community's rivers and drinking water, killing children whose small bodies could not tolerate the arsenic.

The Chinchorro mummies are the oldest artificial mummies in the world—some were created more than a thousand years before the first Egyptian mummies. No one knows for sure why the Chinchorro mummified their children, but some think the grief-stricken community may have sought comfort by preserving their dead. Once they started the practice, the Chinchorro continued to mummify dead people of all ages for centuries to come.

> THE CHINCHORRO PEOPLE MADE MUMMIES FOR MORE THAN 3,000 YEARS, LONGER THAN ANY OTHER CULTURE.

BLACK MUMMIES

The earliest Chinchorro mummies (left) were painted with pigments made from a black mineral called manganese. The Chinchorro used tools such as spears and hooks (far left) to collect food from the sea.

WHO:
DESERT CHILD

CULTURE:
CHINCHORRO

REDISCOVERED:
1917

WHERE:
CHILE

MUMMIFIED:
5050 B.C.

THE PROCESS:

1. Cut off the head and limbs.
2. Take the skin off.
3. Remove the brain.
4. Clean the flesh off the bones.
5. Dry the bones.
6. Put the limbs back together and bind them with sticks, reeds, and grass.
7. Rewrap the limbs with the original skin or bits of seal skin.
8. Hollow out the trunk of the body and dry it with hot ash.
9. Reassemble the whole body with sticks for support.
10. Stuff the body with dry grass or ashes.
11. Cover the body and face with layers of ash paste and make a mask.
12. Attach a wig of human hair.
13. Paint everything black with manganese

FREEZE-DRIED

HIGH-ALTITUDE DISCOVERY
Ötzi's body (above) was found high in the Alps mountain range of Europe (right). It took several days for experts to free his body from the ice (far right) so they could preserve it and solve this mummy mystery.

MURDERED MOUNTAIN MAN

Everyone has heard stories of skiers or hikers who venture into the snowy heights of the Alps, the tallest mountains of Europe, and never come back. Avalanches, sudden snowstorms, or mountain climbing accidents bring their adventures to a deadly end. But an unlucky man who was hiking in the Alps 5,300 years ago met a different kind of death. He was murdered.

Now known as "Ötzi the Iceman," this ill-fated man was trekking along at an elevation of 10,000 feet when an arrow sliced through one of his arteries. He died from blood loss within minutes. Whoever attacked Ötzi was not a robber. Someone, perhaps the killer, took the shaft of the arrow from Ötzi's back but left the victim's valuable goatskin shirt, knife, copper ax, and many other possessions behind. Snow soon covered Ötzi and his belongings. His body wasn't seen again until 1991, when two hikers spotted a corpse partially uncovered as the ice around it melted away.

Ötzi is the oldest frozen human mummy ever found. Researchers have been able to use his body and the well-preserved clothing and artifacts found near him to retrace the story of the Iceman's last few days and hours (read more on pp. 14-15). Yet why he was murdered and who killed him are secrets that may never be revealed.

> ÖTZI, ALSO KNOWN AS "THE ICEMAN," GETS HIS NICKNAME FROM THE ÖTZTAL VALLEY, THE AREA WHERE HE WAS FOUND.

WHO:
ÖTZI THE ICEMAN

CULTURE:
ALPINE COPPER AGE

REDISCOVERED:
1991

WHERE:
ITALY

MUMMIFIED:
ABOUT 3300 B.C.

THE PROCESS:

1. Leave the body at a high altitude, where animals can't get to it.

2. Dry the body in direct sunlight.

3. Freeze the body under ice.

4. Thaw and refreeze many times over 5,000 years.

THE CLUES
More than a dozen arrows like these (far left and center), as well as a copper ax (near left), a six-foot-long bow, clothing, and other equipment were found with Ötzi.

INVESTIGATING THE ICEMAN

An in-depth examination of Ötzi's body helped unravel the mystery of his violent death. But the artifacts found near his body revealed even more valuable information about Ötzi's people, who lived during Europe's Copper Age, from about 3500 B.C. to 1700 B.C. Today Ötzi is stored in a multimillion-dollar refrigerator at the South Tyrol Museum of Archaeology in Italy.

FACE-TO-FACE WITH ÖTZI

National Geographic magazine was the first to reveal what Ötzi might have looked like when he was alive. To re-create the Iceman's face, the magazine launched its own "crime scene investigation," using techniques similar to those police use to identify murder victims—the only difference is that this victim is about 5,300 years old. Following these forensic techniques, an artist put a face on this ancient man.

A stone arrowhead discovered deep within Ötzi's back—shown in this CT scan—cut a major artery, causing him to bleed to death within minutes.

At least a day, if not two or three days, before Ötzi died, he suffered a knife wound to his right hand, the kind one might receive warding off a blow. Could a fight be related to his murder?

1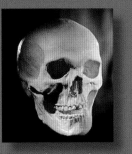

X-rays and computed tomography (CT) scans create 3-D images of Ötzi's head. The artist used this information to sculpt Ötzi's skull in the correct shape.

2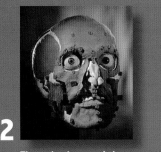

The artist then used clay to create deep muscles and fat, and placed glass eyes in Ötzi's eye sockets. Red tissue depth markers indicate the average amount of flesh over bone for a European, like Ötzi.

3

The markers told the artist how thick to make the skin. No one knows the precise shape of Ötzi's lips, ears, and nose, or the color of his eyes, so the artist had to guess what they might have looked like.

4

The artist created a flexible silicone cast and then painted it the probable skin color of a European living in Ötzi's time. He then added one hair at a time for a final look that is likely similar to Ötzi's actual appearance.

Studies of Ötzi's stomach and intestines show that he had eaten wild goat, red deer, grains, and other plants in the days before he died.

Ötzi was only 40 to 50 years old when he died, but his tough mountain lifestyle made his body look older. A complete examination showed broken ribs, hardened arteries, arthritis, and frostbite in one toe.

Ötzi's legs were strong boned and once big muscled, probably from a lifetime of hiking. Microscopic plant parts found on his clothing and in his gut show that he had been trekking through the Alps in the days before his death, providing further evidence of this mountain lifestyle.

DRIED

DESERT DWELLERS
Many mummies, such as the Beauty of Krorän (above) and a male mummy, wearing a red woolen bracelet (far right), have been found in the desert of China's Tarim Basin (right). Rivers once ran through the area, providing a place for Silk Road travelers to settle and bury their dead.

MUMMIES IN PLAID

The "Beauty of Krorän" is known for her striking auburn hair, narrow face, and pointy nose. But was this mummy a long way from home? Archaeologists discovered the Beauty of Krorän among about 40 other bodies while excavating China's Qäwrighul cemetery in 1979 and 1980. Wrapped in a wool cape and wearing a feathered cap, she was buried with personal items, such as a comb and a straw basket. Her peaceful expression is captivating, but that's not why she drew so much attention.

Like many of the mummies in this cemetery, her features are not typically Chinese. Some of the mummies had reddish or blonde hair and plaid clothing—a style that was unknown in China at the time but identical to patterns seen thousands of miles away in Western Europe. Texts found in the area are also written in languages with Western roots.

> **THE BEAUTY OF KRORÄN'S MUMMIFIED BODY WAS SO DRY THAT IT WEIGHED ONLY 23.5 POUNDS.**

Thousands of years before there were airplanes or cars, how did these people end up here? Experts suspect that the Krorän beauty's culture originated somewhere between Europe and China. Over hundreds of years, the people probably spread out along the Silk Road, a trade route connecting Europe with China. Some traveled west to Europe and others journeyed as far east as the Tarim Basin in China. These wanderers buried the dead near their settlements, where the dry climate preserved their bodies for centuries.

WALKING SHOES
The desert of China's Tarim Basin also preserved the Beauty of Krorän's leather boots (right) and her woven wool cape (opposite, big picture).

WHO:
BEAUTY OF KRORÄN

CULTURE:
TARIM BASIN

REDISCOVERED:
1980

WHERE:
CHINA

MUMMIFIED:
ABOUT 1800 B.C.

THE PROCESS:

1. Clothe the body in a woolen shroud and feathered cap.

2. Place the body in a desert grave.

3. Cover the face and upper torso with a basket.

4. Add a one-foot-deep layer of branches.

5. Add a four-inch-deep layer of reeds.

6. Add a four-inch-deep layer of branches.

7. Cover with dirt and let it sit for 3,800 years.

WRAPPED

VALLEY OF RICHES
Ancient Egypt's most powerful pharaohs were buried
in the Valley of the Kings
(right). The tomb of King Tut
was packed with treasure,
including this famous golden
funerary mask (above) and
a golden collar (far right).

THE GOLDEN PHARAOH

WHO:
PHARAOH
TUTANKHAMUN

CULTURE:
ANCIENT EGYPTIAN

REDISCOVERED:
1922

WHERE:
EGYPT

MUMMIFIED:
1323 B.C.

Archaeologist Howard Carter could not believe his eyes when he peered into the tomb he had just discovered in Egypt's Valley of the Kings. It was filled with statues of strange animals and humans. Carter described how he could see "everywhere the glint of gold." Royal markings stamped on a sealed doorway told him he had found the tomb of Pharaoh Tutankhamun, also known as King Tut. The year was 1922, and no one had been in this room for more than 3,000 years.

In the next room Carter found a box-like golden shrine with three more shrines nested inside it. Within all of these was a heavy granite coffin called a sarcophagus, with three more human-shaped coffins inside. The innermost coffin, made of gleaming solid gold, held King Tut's mummy. The young king—who was only about 19 when he died—was wrapped in linen bandages with a golden helmet-like mask on his head.

KING TUT WAS ONLY NINE YEARS OLD WHEN HE BECAME PHARAOH.

Ancient Egyptians believed that you had to be prepared to have a happy afterlife. So when pharaohs died, they were elaborately mummified and buried with all of their possessions. But grave robbers found their way into almost all of the royal tombs, stealing treasure and moving the mummies. Tut is one of the few royal mummies from ancient Egypt found undisturbed in modern times.

Tut was only about nine years old when he became the pharaoh of Egypt. Much of his life is still a mystery, but the discovery of his tomb provided knowledge about ancient Egypt's culture and royal burials that will live on for an eternity.

BECOMING A KING
Ritual figurines found in Tut's tomb show the pharaoh crowned as King of Upper Egypt (far left) and Lower Egypt (left).

THE PROCESS:

1 Remove all internal organs likely to decay except for the heart. Replace them with linen, sand, or other stuffing to keep the body's shape.

2 Leave the heart—which ancient Egyptians believed to be the center of thought, emotion, and memory—in the body, or take it out, dry it, and then place it back inside the mummy.

3 Punch a hole in the back of the nose or head. Use a long hook like an egg beater to liquefy the brain and pour it out.

4 Wash the body and cover it and the internal organs in a salt called natron for about 70 days until everything is dry.

5 Apply a coating of resins, spices, and ointments to the body and then wrap it from head to toe in linen bandages.

6 Put the dried organs in canisters, called canopic jars, and place them in the tomb near the mummy.

A MUMMY MEETS MODERN SCIENCE

WRAPPED

King Tut's life and death are some of history's greatest mysteries. What did the famous mummy behind the golden mask actually look like? And why did this child-king die when he was only a teenager? Modern technology is beginning to answer some of these age-old questions. In a 2005 investigation led by archaeologist Zahi Hawass, researchers examined Tut's body using a computed tomography (CT) scanner to create a 3-D x-ray of the mummy. Then in 2009, Hawass tested the mummy's DNA. The results have helped the world see what Tut may have looked like when he was alive and shed light on the king's untimely death.

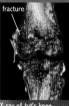

King Tut's mummy

CT scan of Tut's head

fracture

X-ray of tut's knee

MUMMY AUTOPSY

Why did King Tut die so young? Some researchers suggested he had been murdered, killed by a vicious blow to the head. Hawass's team used cutting-edge technology to find out.

A CT scan of his head (above) revealed that what appeared to be a life-threatening injury was actually damage that had taken place after death. In 2009, Hawass's team also discovered that Tut's feet were misshapen, probably as a result of a disease that causes bone tissue to die. The pharaoh's DNA also revealed that he had suffered several bouts of malaria. In this weakened state, an injury such as a broken leg—which some researchers see evidence for in an x-ray of his left knee (above)—could have been the real fatal blow.

A BURIAL FIT FOR A KING

Tut's tomb was carved into the limestone floor of the Valley of the Kings. At the very center of the pharaoh's burial chamber (left) lay a stone sarcophagus with three nested coffins inside that were decorated with gold and inlaid wood (above). The mummy wore a mask of solid gold.

GOING HEAD-TO-HEAD

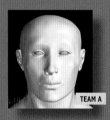

TEAM A

Did Tut look like the golden mask that was found on his mummy (see p. 18)? Three teams of artists and scientists—shown here as Teams A, B, and C—tried to find out. Each team used a digitally generated skull to create a model of Tut. The pharaoh's nose, lips, ears, eye color, skin, and hair were not well-preserved, so no one knows what they really looked like. Still each finished model had similarities. The verdict? None of them looked anything like that world-famous mask.

JOURNEY TO THE AFTERLIFE

(From right to left): A wall painting in Tut's tomb shows a priest in leopard skin preparing the mummy, in white, for the afterlife; Tut being welcomed into the afterlife; Tut embracing the powerful Osiris, lord of the afterlife.

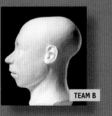

TEAM B   TEAM B

BLIND TEST

TEAM C

Teams A and C were told that the skull belonged to King Tut, but Team B had no idea they were reconstructing the famous pharaoh.

FROZEN

NICE THREADS
The Siberian Ice Maiden (above) was buried in fine clothing. She and her people wore tattoos (see another mummy's skin far right) and were buried under mounds, like these in the Eurasian grasslands (right).

MUMMIES OF THE NOMADS

The body of a young woman was found frozen in a block of ice in 1993. Her internal organs and brain had been removed, and tufts of fur took the place of her eyeballs. She had been buried about 2,500 years earlier in the Altai region of Siberia, beneath a circular mound of rocks known as a *kurgan*. Soon after she was buried, her log burial chamber flooded with water, which then froze, encasing the woman and many of her belongings in ice. This mummy earned the nickname "Siberian Ice Maiden."

Tomb robbers looking for gold had looted most *kurgans* long ago, but they had missed this one. As researchers dug deep into the earth under the rocky mound, they also found the remains of six horses, which were vital to the nomadic culture to which this woman belonged.

THE SIBERIAN ICE MAIDEN IS ALSO KNOWN AS THE "UKOK PRINCESS."

Most of the flesh was lost from her face, but the skin on her shoulders and arms bore tattoos with mythical creatures similar to those seen in the jewelry and textiles of other nomadic Scytho-Siberian groups, who lived in the grasslands between the Black Sea and Siberia from 800 B.C. to 300 B.C.

Archaeologists are concerned that as the world's climate warms up, frozen tombs remaining in these grasslands might melt. This means that the mummies would decay, making it only a matter of time before the bodies disappear forever.

ANIMAL ART
Graceful animals, some mythical and some real, appear in this culture's artwork. On a saddle (above left) found in a tomb, a fictional eagle-griffin attacks an ibex—a type of wild goat. A golden elk plaque (left) was found thousands of miles to the west near the Black Sea.

WHO:
SIBERIAN ICE MAIDEN

CULTURE:
SCYTHO-SIBERIAN

REDISCOVERED:
1993

WHERE:
RUSSIA

MUMMIFIED:
ABOUT 500 B.C.

THE PROCESS:

1 Slice open the belly and take out the internal organs.

2 Remove the brain through the back of the skull.

3 Stuff the corpse with bark and a spongy soil called peat.

4 Remove the eyeballs and replace them with fur.

5 Place the body in a hollowed-out log in an underground chamber.

6 Flood the chamber with water.

7 Freeze the water for 2,500 years.

TANNED

REST IN PEAT
Many cultures dumped their unwanted dead, like the hanged Tollund Man (above), in marshy bogs (right). Today archaeologists excavate bodies from peat, the dried out remains of the bogs (far right).

BODIES FROM THE BOGS

WHO:
TOLLUND MAN

CULTURE:
NORTHERN EUROPEAN
IRON AGE

REDISCOVERED:
1950

WHERE:
DENMARK

MUMMIFIED:
ABOUT 400 B.C.

When Danish farmers stumbled across a dead man in a bog with a rope around his neck, they called the police. But the police soon realized that this murder mystery could only be solved by archaeologists. The body was roughly 2,400 years old.

"Tollund Man," named after Tollund Fen where he was found, is a bog body—one of the most unusual types of mummies in the world. These bodies are found in rich soil called peat, which is the dried remains of marshy bogs that existed centuries earlier. The majority of these people had been strangled, hanged, tortured, or had their throats slit, and were then tossed into the muck. The bogs preserved their bodies so well that you can often see pores in their skin and beard stubble on the male mummies' faces.

PEAT DIGGERS—PEOPLE WHO COLLECT THE BOGS' RICH SOIL—DISCOVER MANY OF THE BOG BODIES.

We do not know what led to these violent deaths, but historical records left by the Romans—who traded and fought with the tribes of northern Europe during the first four centuries A.D.—tell us that local people practiced human sacrifice and punished criminals in ways that could have led to these grisly killings.

What we do know is that many ancient European cultures considered bogs—where mist rises, trees rock, and you can fall through the ground into the thick black water below—to be the place where world of the living met the world of the dead.

THE PROCESS:

1. Place the body in cold water to slow decay and keep insects away.

2. Make sure the water is low in oxygen so bacteria can't advance decay.

3. Pin the body down so it doesn't float away.

4. Let the water's natural tannins—a substance from plants that is used to tan animal hides—give the body a leathery texture.

IRON AGE TREASURES
A 2,000-year-old silver cauldron (detail shown left) and 2,300-year-old shoes (above left) are among many artifacts found in northern Europe's peat bogs.

25

TALES FROM THE BOGS

If you have a weak stomach, you might want to stop here! Bog bodies, found from Ireland to Russia, often belonged to criminals, outcasts, and sacrificial victims who met gruesome deaths. Little did the killers or victims know that thousands of years later these deaths would help us understand their lives and cultures.

CLONYCAVAN MAN

Discovered in central Ireland in 2005, "Clonycavan Man" met his tragic fate about 2,000 years ago. His insides were torn out before he was chopped three times in the head with an ax. His styled hair hints that he may have been a noble, perhaps executed for breaking a code of honor.

RED FRANZ

Named for his flame-colored hair and beard, "Red Franz" probably had blond hair, though it's been tinted red by the bog. Found in 1900 in Germany, the body had a slit throat and was thought to be a modern murder victim. It took five months for authorities to realize that the crime had occured 1,600 years earlier.

GRAUBALLE MAN

One of the best preserved of the bog bodies, 2,300-year-old "Grauballe Man" still has his hair and beard stubble, and his fingerprints are clearly visible. He was found near Grauballe, Denmark, in 1952. Researchers once thought that the man's fractured skull, broken leg, and slit throat were evidence of torture. Later experts discovered that pressure in the bog caused two of these injuries after death. Fatally cut from ear-to-ear, the man may have been part of a sacrifice to a fertility goddess.

BOG TREASURES

Human bodies are not the only things that bogs preserve. Many objects found in the peat were ritual offerings, made by people asking their gods for help. Other objects (and even animals) may have fallen in by accident. Musical instruments, bunches of human hair, weapons, and gold have all been pulled out of the soil. Here is a look at just a few of the objects that have been recovered from bogs in northern Europe.

Necklace, Denmark, 600 B.C.

YDE GIRL

This 2,000-year-old body of a teenage girl was found in a peat bog near the village of Yde, Netherlands, in 1897. Her body was damaged when it was removed from the bog, but her shawl and hair were well preserved. The girl had a knife wound in her chest and a woolen cord around her neck—convincing evidence that she had been murdered.

Bronze horse and chariot, Denmark, 1400 B.C.

Drinking horn, Denmark, A.D. 400

Bog dog, Germany, A.D. 1550

27

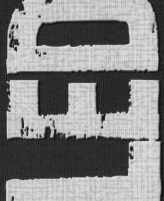

BURIED

MYSTERIOUS PACKAGE
The mummy of the Lady of Cao (above) was found inside this burial bundle (right) at the ancient ruins of El Brujo in Peru. She was buried with many weapons and a copper bowl on her face (far right).

WARRIOR WOMAN

WHO:
LADY OF CAO

CULTURE:
MOCHE

REDISCOVERED:
2005

WHERE:
PERU

MUMMIFIED:
ABOUT A.D. 400

THE PROCESS:

1 Cover the body in cinnabar (a red-colored mercury ore).

2 Wrap the body in hundreds of yards of cloth.

3 Place meaningful objects within the bundle as you wrap.

4 Leave the body deep within an adobe tomb and let the body dry out for 1,600 years.

Everything about a tomb discovered inside a pyramid in Peru indicated that a powerful man was buried inside. But a surprise lay deep within this 1,600-year-old grave.

Pyramid burials were nothing new at this sacred site, called El Brujo, where the warfaring Moche culture gave their VIPs elaborate burials. Like many other Moche mummies, the body was wrapped in hundreds of yards of cloth strips, and a sacrificial victim lay nearby. Two large war clubs and 28 spear throwers were included in the noble's bundle, along with golden nose rings, headdresses, necklaces of tiny human heads, and other symbols of power.

THIS MUMMY LOOKS LIKE IT'S SCREAMING, BUT ITS OPEN MOUTH IS ACTUALLY CAUSED BY THE LOOSENING AND THEN STIFFENING OF MUSCLES THAT OCCURS A FEW HOURS AFTER DEATH.

As researchers carefully unwound the cloth, the investigation took a stunning turn. They found weaving tools, sewing needles, and raw cotton inside—items typically associated with Moche women. When they lifted a gilded copper bowl covering its face, they were shocked to find that the mummy was a woman in her late twenties. She had long braids, and her arms and legs were covered in animal tattoos. The researchers nicknamed her "Lady of Cao" after her burial pyramid, called *Huaca de Cao Viejo*.

For the first time, it was clear that Moche women held positions of power. So who was this mystery mummy? Was she a priestess? A warrior queen? Her true identity is still waiting to be uncovered.

ROYAL TATTOOS
Snake, seahorse, and spider tattoos slither and crawl up the Moche mummy's arms (far right). Her culture also made beautiful art, such as this figurine (below).

MUMMIES, MUMMIES, EVERYWHERE

The Moche were just one of Peru's many mummy-making cultures. According to reports by the conquering Spanish in the 1500s, the ancient Inca mummified their emperors and took care of them in palaces as if they were still alive. On special days, they dressed the mummies in royal garments and paraded them through the streets. Not all mummies were royalty. Bundling mummies was common practice in Peru, and the country's dry environment created many mummies naturally.

CHACHAPOYA

Northern Peru was the home of the Chachapoya, also called the "Cloud People," because they lived in a misty mountain environment. Between about A.D. 750 and A.D. 1400, the Chachapoya mummified their dead, removing internal organs, draining body fluids, and sometimes placing offerings of coca leaves with the bodies. They stored the bodies in dry caves and cliffs, where they were preserved for thousands of years.

CHIRIBAYA

The Chiribaya culture thrived in southern Peru between A.D. 900 and A.D. 1300. They placed their dead in crouched positions, wrapped them with brightly colored textiles and ropes, and buried them in deep pits. The dry climate preserved many items placed in the tombs, such as baskets, leather objects, food, and feathers.

INCA ICE MAIDEN

Perhaps Peru's most famous mummy, "Juanita," also called the "Inca Ice Maiden" (left) was sacrificed in a ritual when she was just 14 years old. Juanita was killed on a platform built 20,000 feet high in the Andes Mountains. Priests placed her body in a small pit along with burial goods, such as shells and a small llama statue (below). The cold, dry environment on the mountain preserved her body for some 500 years.

INCA CEMETERY

More than 2,200 bundled mummies were found at Puruchuco, an archaeological site in Lima, Peru. Buried in an Inca cemetery dating back to the late 1400s, the mummies were spread out across an area as large as five football fields. Some of the bodies were well-preserved in bundles (far right), while skeletons (below) were all that remained of others.

SEALED

ALL DRESSED UP
Eung Tae's mummy (above and right) was buried in a coffin with many articles of clothing (far right). No one knows how he died, but researchers are studying the mummies in this cemetery for signs of disease.

KOREAN TIME CAPSULES

WHO:
EUNG TAE

CULTURE:
JOSEON DYNASTY

REDISCOVERED:
1998

WHERE:
KOREA

MUMMIFIED:
1586

THE PROCESS:

1 Bundle the body in textiles tied with hemp rope.

2 Place the body and textiles inside two thick pine coffins, each separated by a layer of charcoal.

3 Place a mixture of lime and dirt around the coffin.

4 When water contacts this soil mixture, it will become hard, like a concrete jacket.

5 Leave it in the ground for 400 years.

"You always said we would be living together to die on the same day. However, why did you go to heaven alone? Why did you go alone, leaving our child and me behind?" This sad note, written by a mourning widow in 1586, was buried with the mummy of her husband, a Korean man named Eung Tae.

Four hundred years later, construction workers in the South Korean city of Andong stumbled upon a tomb filled with mummies. When they opened one of the graves, Eung Tae's well-preserved body and grave revealed a personal record of his life and times. His grave—preserved by adding a mineral called lime to the soil—included 72 items of beautiful clothing, including clothes belonging to his wife and their child. He was also buried with letters from his relatives and a pair of sandals made from his wife's hair—a traditional cure for illness. Eung Tae's grave was filled with clues to the past. But scientists had to investigate quickly.

EUNG TAE'S STORY INSPIRED AT LEAST TWO NOVELS, A SONG, A PLAY, AND AN OPERA.

Koreans from this time period, the Joseon Dynasty, had great respect for their ancestors and wanted them to be happy in the afterlife. Many modern Koreans share those feelings and do not want their ancestors disturbed. Eung Tae's tomb was reburied the same day it was excavated.

From the mementos left in his grave, researchers were able to weave together the sad story of a man struck with a fatal illness and taken from his loving family too soon.

LOVE STORY
Eung Tae's wife placed these sandals woven from her own hair in the coffin, along with letters expressing her grief (left).

DRAINED

ISLAND OF MUMMIES
A mummified clergyman (above) earned a special place in the crypt of the Cathedral of Novara di Sicilia (right). This body is one of many mummies on the island of Sicily, Italy, including those in the Capuchin catacombs (far right).

CLERGY IN THE CRYPTS

WHO:
A CLERGYMAN

CULTURE:
SICILIAN ROMAN
CATHOLIC

REDISCOVERED:
1990s

WHERE:
ITALY

MUMMIFIED:
19TH CENTURY

A hidden chamber lies beneath the altar of a beautiful cathedral on the island of Sicily, Italy. Press a button and the floor opens, revealing a spooky chamber where six religious leaders are nestled in alcoves in the stone walls. They look almost alive, until you see the dried flesh and bone poking out of their garments. Located in the town of Novara di Sicilia, these honored clergymen lived more than a hundred years ago. When they died, their bodies were mummified as a sign of respect. A floor was built over the entrance to the crypts, probably in the mid-20th century. The tomb remained a secret until it was rediscovered in the 1990s.

All over Sicily, people had unusual ways of caring for the dead. Not far away from Novara Di Sicilia, in the catacombs of the Capuchin monastery in Palermo, about 1,800 lifelike bodies hang on the walls, sit on benches, and lean casually, as if they're waiting for the bus (inset, opposite page). Except that some of them have been waiting for as long as 400 years.

The dry, cool air of the underground chamber naturally mummified the monks who were interred there. Later the monastery invited wealthy citizens to bury their dead there as well. Many of these mummies still wear the clothing—now in shreds—that their families dressed them in when they died. Experts continue to hunt for mummies in crypts all across the island.

> A SICILIAN MUMMY EXPERT RECENTLY DISCOVERED THE SECRET EMBALMING RECIPE USED IN THE CAPUCHIN CATACOMBS.

THE PROCESS:

1. Place the corpse in a special mummifying room, called a crypt, in a sitting position over a bowl-shaped drain.

2. Allow body fluids to slowly leak out and permit the flesh to dry.

3. When it's dry, place the body upright for display. Use a stick inside the body for artificial support if necessary.

4. If desired, stuff with herbs to reduce the odors of decay.

5. Leave it in the crypt for 200 years.

THE DEAD LIVE ON
In the Capuchin catacombs, the dead seem eerily alive. The parents of two-year-old Rosalia Lombardo (far left) had their daughter embalmed after her death in 1920. Today, she still looks like she's sleeping. A scarlet-caped mummy of a priest (left) appears to be deep in prayer.

EMBALMED

HISTORY ON DISPLAY
Lenin's body (above) has been on display in a mausoleum in Moscow, Russia, for almost a hundred years. The leader of the Russian Revolution, Lenin addressed crowds in Moscow's Red Square in October 1917 (right).

CELEBRITY MUMMIES

WHO:
VLADIMIR LENIN

CULTURE:
SOVIET RUSSIAN

WHERE:
RUSSIA

MUMMIFIED:
1924

Vladimir Lenin was the George Washington of the Soviet Union, the communist empire that unified Russia and 14 other countries in Asia and Eastern Europe for most of the 20th century. When Lenin died in 1924, scientists were asked to prepare Lenin's body for "all eternity." The corpse was artificially mummified in a process called embalming and placed on public display. Leaders believed that the body of the Soviet Union's founding father would be an inspiration for generations to come.

Lenin and the leader who followed him, Josef Stalin, were mummified in great secrecy. Anyone who revealed these secrets would face certain death. Although millions of people paraded past these bodies, for decades no one knew how their lifelike appearance was maintained.

The secret remained as well preserved as the two leaders' bodies until 1989, when the Soviet Union collapsed. Lenin's and Stalin's popularity slipped, and it wasn't long before Ilya Zbarsky, the scientist in charge maintaining their bodies, revealed the secret recipe.

While the bodies of leaders like these can be preserved for decades, positive feelings toward them may not last. Countless tombs of once-beloved leaders have been looted or destroyed when the leaders fell out of favor. For a mummy, politics can be more dangerous than the ravages of time.

> ABRAHAM LINCOLN'S EMBALMED BODY WAS EXHUMED 36 YEARS AFTER HE WAS BURIED AND FOUND TO BE INTACT.

THE PROCESS:

1. Inject the body with a top-secret chemical formula.
2. Bathe the body every 18 months in the secret formula.
3. Daub the exposed parts of the body with embalming fluid twice a week.
4. Keep the body in a temperature-controlled, airtight glass coffin.

THE DEAD ON DISPLAY
Jeremy Bentham (above), a 19th-century philosopher, asked to be mummified. His skeleton and a replica of his mummified head are on display in London, England. The mummy of St. Zita (right), the patron saint of domestic servants who died in 1272, is on display in Italy.

SMOKED

HANGING OUT
Mummified village chief Moimango (above) was displayed in a chair suspended from a cliff wall for decades. He was one of the last mummies made by the Anga tribe, who live in the Papua New Guinea highlands (right).

THE MAN WHO WANTS TO BE A MUMMY

Mummies watch over the small village of Koke, Papua New Guinea. Perched under a rock shelter on a cliff, the mummies bring comfort to the Anga people, who respect these mummies and treat them as if they are alive. But there hasn't been a new mummy since former village chief Moimango died around 1950.

Mummification is common in New Guinea and other islands of Melanesia, but Christian missionaries discouraged Anga burial rituals because they involve beliefs in ghosts and spirits. Soon this cultural knowledge started slipping away.

THE ANGA PEOPLE ARE ALSO CALLED THE KUKUKUKU.

Now Moimango's son and current village chief, Gematsu, wants to restore this ancient ritual. In keeping with tradition, Gematsu mummified Moimango when he died. Gematsu's dream is to have the same honor. When he dies, Gematsu wants to become a mummy.

To bring back the tradition in time for his own death, Gematsu taught some younger Anga, including his son, how to preserve and make mummies like their ancestors had—by smoking the corpses. They built a special shelter called a smoking hut and used the method at right to mummify a dead pig for practice. Gematsu's son watched carefully. Now when the time comes, he can mummify his father and revive this cherished tradition.

THE SMOKEHOUSE
A hut for smoking corpses was constructed on the outskirts of the village. For practice, villagers mummified a dead pig.

WHO:
CHIEF MOIMANGO

CULTURE:
ANGA

REDISCOVERED:
2008

WHERE:
PAPUA NEW GUINEA

MUMMIFIED:
ABOUT 1950

THE PROCESS:

1 Construct a ceremonial smoking hut of palm leaves and bamboo during a three- to five-day mourning period.

2 In the smoking hut, scrape the corpse's skin and hair with a plant bristle brush and bamboo.

3 Gently squeeze fluids through the skin to help dry the body.

4 Place the body in a chair made from branches and keep a smoky fire going for about 30 days. Keep brushing and squeezing out fluids.

5 Put red ochre clay on the body. This helps draw out more fluids.

6 Dress the mummy in a grass skirt and cap and place on a cliff ledge where there is a nice breeze.

SMOKED
MUMMY REPAIR SHOP

Chief Moimango's mummy was falling apart. Like other Anga mummies (below, right), it had sat outside for decades. Skin was peeling off his skull, and his fingers and toes were overgrown with plant life and were starting to fall off. A rodent had made a hole in the mummy's stomach, and wasps had nested in his head. But no one in the Anga tribe knew how to fix him. So Gematsu asked American mummy expert Ronald Beckett to teach his people how to put this treasured mummy back together again.

IT'S A WRAP
An Anga villager wraps rope made from tree bark around Moimango's leg to help hold his fragile body together.

ALL PATCHED UP
Beckett examined the mummy to learn about Moimango's way of life (left) and showed Moimango's son and other tribe members how to repair the body using materials from the surrounding jungle. They used bamboo brushes to clean the mummy, tree sap (below) to glue the skin to the skull, and a material made from tree bark to patch holes and stabilize the head. The finishing touch? A layer of orange ochre mud to give the mummy a protective coating.

LOOKING GOOD
Moimango, now a spruced-up mummy, took his old place in a rock shelter on a cliff (left). Gematsu (center) and his son Awateng sit nearby. One day Awateng will have the honor of preserving his father as a mummy.

MUMMIES THROUGH THE AGES

Each mummy featured in this book is a human time capsule. When modern-day scientists unwrap a mummy bundle for the first time or dig up a preserved ancient body, long-lost secrets from the past are revealed. How the body was buried, and the mummy's clothing, hairstyle, and personal possessions all provide a snapshot of the person's life and culture. This time line shows when the mummified people in this book lived in relation to the amount of time their cultures existed.* Each mummy preserves only a brief moment in its culture's history.

BEAUTY OF KRORÄN
China
ABOUT 1800 B.C.

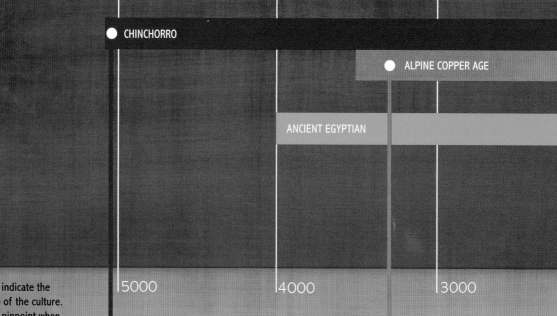

CHINCHORRO

ALPINE COPPER AGE

ANCIENT EGYPTIAN

*Color bars indicate the
date range of the culture.
White dots pinpoint when
the mummy lived.

5000   4000   3000   2000

DESERT CHILD
Chile
5050 B.C.

ÖTZI THE ICEMAN
Italy
About 3300 B.C.

**PHARAOH
TUTANKHAMUN**
Egypt
1323 B.C.

42

SIBERIAN ICE MAIDEN
Russia
ABOUT 500 B.C.

LADY OF CAO
Peru
ABOUT A.D. 400

EUNG TAE
Korea
A.D. 1586

CHIEF MOIMANGO
Papua New Guinea
ABOUT 1950

***The start date of the Anga culture is unknown. The Anga tribe still exists today.

TARIM BASIN

ANGA***

JOSEON DYNASTY

SCYTHO-SIBERIAN

SICILIAN ROMAN CATHOLIC****

BOG BODIES**

SOVIET UNION

MOCHE

1000   **B.C. | A.D.**   1000   2000

TOLLUND MAN
Denmark
ABOUT 400 B.C.

**Various Northern European Iron Age cultures

CLERGYMAN
Italy
19TH CENTURY

****The Sicilian Roman Catholic culture still thrives today.

VLADIMIR LENIN
Russia
1924

A WORLD OF MUMMIES

When most people think of mummies, they think of ancient Egypt. But both man-made and natural mummies are found on every continent in the world, except for Antarctica. On this map, you'll find the world's oldest man-made mummy, preserved in Chile more than 3,600 years before King Tut was born! You can also locate the oldest human mummy of all time—a naturally preserved body mummified in 7415 B.C. in what is now Nevada. Take this quick tour of some of the most fascinating mummies on Earth.

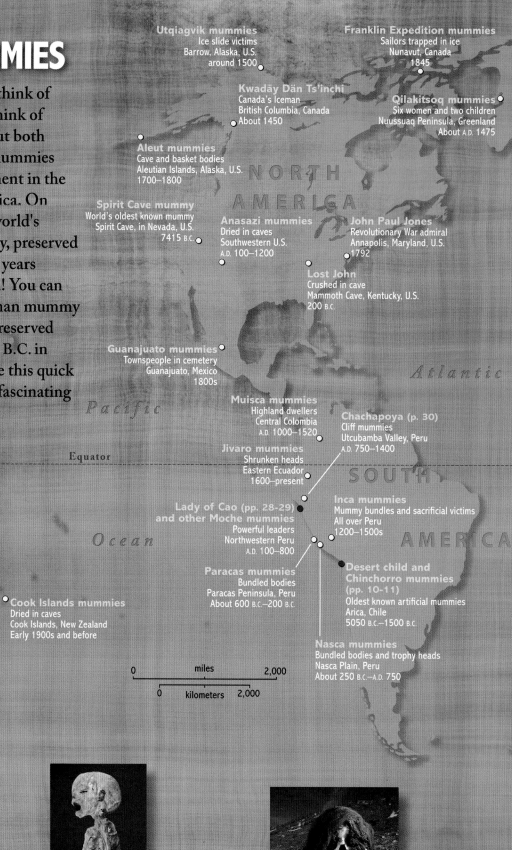

Utqiagvik mummies
Ice slide victims
Barrow, Alaska, U.S.
around 1500

Franklin Expedition mummies
Sailors trapped in ice
Nunavut, Canada
1845

Kwadāy Dän Ts'ínchi
Canada's Iceman
British Columbia, Canada
About 1450

Qilakitsoq mummies
Six women and two children
Nuussuaq Peninsula, Greenland
About A.D. 1475

Aleut mummies
Cave and basket bodies
Aleutian Islands, Alaska, U.S.
1700–1800

NORTH AMERICA

Spirit Cave mummy
World's oldest known mummy
Spirit Cave, in Nevada, U.S.
7415 B.C.

Anasazi mummies
Dried in caves
Southwestern U.S.
A.D. 100–1200

John Paul Jones
Revolutionary War admiral
Annapolis, Maryland, U.S.
1792

Lost John
Crushed in cave
Mammoth Cave, Kentucky, U.S.
200 B.C.

Guanajuato mummies
Townspeople in cemetery
Guanajuato, Mexico
1800s

Atlantic

Pacific

Muisca mummies
Highland dwellers
Central Colombia
A.D. 1000–1520

Chachapoya (p. 30)
Cliff mummies
Utcubamba Valley, Peru
A.D. 750–1400

Equator

Jivaro mummies
Shrunken heads
Eastern Ecuador
1600–present

SOUTH

Lady of Cao (pp. 28–29) and other Moche mummies
Powerful leaders
Northwestern Peru
A.D. 100–800

Inca mummies
Mummy bundles and sacrificial victims
All over Peru
1200–1500s

Ocean

AMERICA

Paracas mummies
Bundled bodies
Paracas Peninsula, Peru
About 600 B.C.–200 B.C.

Desert child and Chinchorro mummies (pp. 10–11)
Oldest known artificial mummies
Arica, Chile
5050 B.C.–1500 B.C.

Cook Islands mummies
Dried in caves
Cook Islands, New Zealand
Early 1900s and before

Nasca mummies
Bundled bodies and trophy heads
Nasca Plain, Peru
About 250 B.C.–A.D. 750

miles
0   2,000

0   kilometers   2,000

Mummified baby
Guanajuato,
Mexico

Nasca mummy
Nasca Plain, Peru

Tollund Man and other bog bodies (pp. 24-27)
Northern Europe, including Tollund Man in Denmark
About 400 B.C.–A.D. 400

Vladimir Lenin (pp. 36-37)
Founder of Soviet Union
Moscow, Russia
1924

Siberian Ice Maiden (pp. 22-23)
Noble nomad
Siberia, Russia
About 500 B.C.

Eung Tae (pp. 32-33) and other Korean mummies
Medieval nobility
Andong, Korea
16th–17th century

Jeremy Bentham (p. 37)
British philosopher
England, U.K.
1832

Ötzi the Iceman (pp. 12-15)
Europe's oldest mummy
Ötztal valley, in Italy
3300 B.C.

Salt mummies
Victims of mine collapse
Zanjan, Iran
About 550 B.C.–A.D. 650

Mao Zedong
Founder of People's Republic of China
Beijing, China
1976

Fujiwara mummies
Japanese chieftains
Honshu, Japan
About A.D. 1100

Italian saints
Catholic church figures
All over Italy
About 13th century–present

Beauty of Krorän (pp. 16-17) and other Tarim Basin mummies
Silk Road settlers
China
About 1800 B.C.–A.D. 400

Buddhist monks
Religious mummies
Japan, Thailand, Vietnam
1300–1990

Guanche mummies
Dried in caves
Canary Islands, Spain
A.D. 400–1500

King Tut (pp. 18-21) and other Egyptian mummies
Royal and noble tombs
Egypt, including King Tut in Luxor
About 4000 B.C.–about A.D. 400

Ho Chi Minh
Founder of modern Vietnam
Hanoi, Vietnam
1969

Libyan mummy
Sahara desert child
Central Libya
3455 B.C.

Ibaloy mummies
Fire-dried bodies
Benguet Province, Philippines
1500–1800

Clergyman and other Sicilian mummies (pp. 34-35)
In catacombs and crypts
Sicily, Italy
1599–1920

Chief Moimango and Anga mummies (pp. 38-41)
Smoked cliff bodies
Papua New Guinea
19th century (or earlier)–about 1950

Torres Strait mummies
Decorated with red pigment and shells
Queensland, Australia
Early 1900s and before

Australian mummies
Mummified in fetal position
Queensland, Australia
Early 1900s and before

Arctic Ocean

EUROPE

ASIA

AFRICA

Equator

Indian Ocean

Ocean

Ocean

AUSTRALIA

Map Key

○————— Location of mummy
●————— Mummy featured in this book

King Tut (pp. 18-21) and other Egyptian mummies ————— Name of mummy or group of mummies
Royal and noble tombs ————— Description
Egypt, including King Tut in Luxor ————— Where found
About 4000 B.C.–about A.D. 400 ————— When the bodies were mummified

Maori
Tattooed heads
New Zealand
1600s (or earlier)–1800s

Pharaoh Ramses II
Egypt

Tarim Basin mummy
Tarim Basin, China

Mummified monk
Ko Samui, Thailand

GLOSSARY

A.D.: an abbreviation for "anno Domini," meaning "year of the Lord." This is used to designate a time division between Christian and pre-Christian times. Our calendar years are based on the division between A.D. and B.C. (see B.C.). Another term sometimes used instead of A.D. is C.E., meaning the "common era."

ARTERIES: tube-like vessels in the body that take blood from the heart to the rest of the body

BACTERIA: single-celled microorganisms that live almost everywhere on Earth, including on and within human bodies

B.C.: an abbreviation for "before Christ," used to designate time before the Christian era. Another term sometimes used instead of B.C. is B.C.E., which means "before common era."

COMPUTED TOMOGRAPHY (CT): a medical imaging technology that uses multiple x-rays to create 3-D images. This technology is particularly good at imaging dense bone against soft tissues.

CAPUCHIN: a Catholic religious order founded in 1529

CATACOMBS: an underground cemetery, often with many corridors and niches for the dead

COPPER AGE: the period when cultures used copper alone, before it was mixed with tin to make bronze. Different cultures used copper at different times.

CORPSE: a dead body

CRYPT: an underground chamber, usually under a church

DECAY: in human bodies, this is the process of decomposition, which is aided by bacteria. The end result of decay is the return of the whole body to the earth.

DECOMPOSITION: in bodies, this is the breaking apart of the body into its original parts, such as chemicals.

EMBALM: to stop the decay of a body. There are many different embalming treatments.

FETAL POSITION: a crouched position with legs brought up tightly against the chest. This is the position of an unborn child, or fetus, in the womb, and is

sometimes the position in which mummies are buried.

MUMMY: mummified human remains of any sort, but usually a corpse with enough soft tissue preserved on it to resemble a person rather than a skeleton

NOMADS: people who move from place to place, often accompanied by their livestock. Their movement is often linked to finding good pastures.

PEAT: a rich soil composed of the remains of plants found in swamps and bogs. It can be used as fertilizer or burned as fuel.

SACRIFICE: to offer something precious, sometimes in exchange for something. For example, offering the life of a victim to a deity in exchange for better weather.

SARCOPHAGUS: a stone coffin (The word means "flesh-eating stone" in Greek.)

SCYTHO-SIBERIAN: a cultural group that includes the influence of the Scythians near the Black Sea in Eurasia and faraway people, such as the Pazyryk, from Siberia. This culture lasted from about 1800 B.C. to A.D. 400.

AUTHOR'S NOTE

This book was produced out of a real passion for mummies. I want the world to see them not as odd curiosities, but as real people who lived in the past and have much to tell us. Until mummies are better understood, many will continue to suffer damage from neglect.

The chapters in this book reflect the work of many dedicated researchers who introduced me to the world of mummies. Among these, I would like to thank Bernardo Arriaza of the University of Nevada, Arthur Aufderheide of the University of Minnesota, Ronald Beckett of Quinnipiac University, Dong Hoon Shin of Seoul National University, Heather Gill-Robinson of the Reiss-Engelhorn Museum, Zahi Hawass of Egypt's Supreme Council of Antiquities, Esther Jacobson-Tepfer of the University of Oregon, Janice Kamrin of the American Research Center in Egypt, Victor H. Mair of the University of Pennsylvania, Dario Piombino-Mascali and Albert Zink of the Institute for Mummies and the Iceman, Johan Reinhard of the Mountain Institute, Frank Rühli of the University of Zurich, Calogera Santoro of the Universidad de Tarapacá, and Se Gweon Yim of the Andong University Museum. Thank you to Dr. Christina Elson at *National Geographic* magazine for reviewing the text. Finally, without the support of my family, this book would not have been possible.

BIBLIOGRAPHY

ARTICLES IN *NATIONAL GEOGRAPHIC*

Cock, Guillermo A. *Inca Rescue.* May 2002.

Gill, A. A. *Where the Dead Don't Sleep: Sicily's Mummies.* February 2009.

Hall, Stephen S. *Last Hours of the Iceman.* July 2007.

Lange, Karen E. *Tales from the Bog.* September 2007.

Williams, A. R. *Modern Technology Reopens the Ancient Case of King Tut.* June 2005.

Williams, A. R. *Mystery of the Tattooed Mummy.* June 2006.

BOOKS

Aufderheide, A.C. *The Scientific Study of Mummies.* Cambridge University Press, 2003.

Bahn, P. *Tombs, Graves and Mummies.* Barnes & Noble, Inc., 1996.

Cockburn, A., Cockburn, E., and Reyman, T. A. *Mummies, Disease and Ancient Cultures.* Cambridge University Press, 1998.

Glob, P. V. *The Bog People.* New York Review Books, 1965.

Mallory, J. P. and Mair, V. H. *The Tarim Mummies.* Thames & Hudson Ltd., 2000.

Moseley, M. *The Incas and Their Ancestors.* Thames & Hudson Ltd., 2001.

Parker Pearson, M. *The Archaeology of Death and Burial.* Texas A & M University Press, 2001.

Reinhard, J. *Inca Ice Maiden.* National Geographic Society, 1998.

Sloan, C. *Bury the Dead: Tombs, Corpses, Mummies, Skeletons, and Rituals.* National Geographic, 2002.

Toby Evans, Susan. *Ancient Mexico and Central America.* Thames & Hudson Ltd., 2004.

WEB SITES

Learn about mummies around the world. mummytombs.com/main.locator.htm

Examine the body of Ötzi the Iceman on this interactive site. ngm.nationalgeographic.com/2007/0 iceman/iceman-graphic-interactive

Take a 360-degree interactive tour of King Tut's tomb. ngm.nationalgeographic.com/2005/06/ king-tut/mysteries/home

ILLUSTRATION CREDITS

INDEX